True Shoals Ghost Stories
Stories
Vol. 2

DEBRA GLASS

To Patricia Happy thunting! Debra Glass

ISBN: 151464553X
ISBN-13: 978-1514645536

DEDICATION

For Julie.

CONTENTS

Acknowledgments   i

The Ghost of the Sheffield Post Office   3

The Lady Spirit of Coby Hall   7

The Coffee-Reisman House Haunting   17

Spooks in the Nance Home   27

The Pickett Place Poltergeist   31

The Spirits of Sweetwater Mansion   37

Violet   45

The Ghosts of Woodlawn Plantation   49

The Hollerin' Thang   61

Randolph of the Ritz   67

George   73

Haunted Florence Cemetery   77

Pope's Tavern   85

ACKNOWLEDGMENTS

I would like to thank the following people for the generous contributions to my stories: Fay Abramson, Zac Abramson, Gina Bailey, Bill Bland, Carole Bland, Todd Bradford, Karen Christian, Gerald Clemmons, Addie Doty, Lee Freeman, Norma Glascock, Elizabeth "Tudy" Herston, Jimmie Hills, Deborah Hinton, David Hope, Rick Hyde, Jeanette McClure PhD, Betty McCreless, William McDonald, Donald Murks, Jimmy Oliver, Terry Pace, Jo Parkhurst, Lettie Region, John Rice MD, Joe Slate PhD, Joyce Sons, Favre Sparks, Donna Burns Sparks, Gilbert Terry, John Terry, Bobbie Tomsik, Marilyn Watson, Charlotte West, Benji Wilson, Rilly Winkle, and Geneva Yerbey.

Special thanks to my mother, Sandra Calvert Terry, for helping me to realize my dreams. To Granny – Gracie Stutts, who proofread for me.

And to Karen Murphy Merrigan, my best friend since fifth grade at Underwood School.

Cover Art by Tricia "Pickyme" Schmitt
Back cover author photo by Mary Carton

THE GHOST OF THE SHEFFIELD POST OFFICE

When Rick Hyde transferred to the Sheffield Post Office from the Florence Post Office, in the early 1990s, he didn't know one of his fellow employees would turn out to be a ghost.

One morning around 5:45 am, he and several other postal workers were facing the box section and sorting mail. Rick was working, his attention focused on the letters in front of him when he noticed a sudden drop in temperature. He shuddered and out of the corner of his eye, caught the figure of a man walking toward the carrier cases. That seemed odd since no one else was supposed to be in the building except two other coworkers who were occupied beside him. He glanced up to see who it was and, to his horror, he watched as the man walked straight through the carrier case.

He blinked and stared, certain of what he'd just witnessed. "Who just walked past me?" he demanded, trying to sort of the strange sight in his head.

"Nobody," the others told him.

"Oh yes, there was," Rick declared vehemently. "I saw a man about six feet tall with sandy hair and wire rimmed glasses. He had on a pair of carrier pants with stripes down the legs."

Rick's coworkers looked at each other, their eyes wide. "Carl," they said in unison.

The Sheffield Post Office was founded sometime in the 1880s, during the industrial boom in Sheffield when the furnaces, iron related factories, and railroad came to the area. The present post office was constructed in 1929, by the Samford Brothers contractors and is located at 210 Columbia Avenue in downtown Sheffield.

Carl, as the legend is told, was a mail carrier at the Sheffield Post Office. Apparently, the old adage that neither rain, sleet, nor snow will stop a postal carrier holds true, even in death. Almost all the employees there have seen Carl's apparition going about his day to day duties.

Rick Hyde has seen Carl several times. Once, he started around the corner to go up the stairs and suddenly, he came face to face with Carl's ghost. Carl was casually sitting on the stairs, about half way up the flight.

Rick stopped in his tracks and stared. "Hello, Carl," he said after his initial shock.

Carl simply smiled, stood up, and then vanished.

The Sheffield Post Office

The post master, Hugh Robinson, also had an experience with

Carl. One morning he was on the workroom floor, sorting through the mail when, out of the corner of his eye, he noticed a man coming toward him. He looked up and the man disappeared.

Having heard the stories about Carl, Hugh told his coworkers what he'd seen and described the man as having sandy hair and wearing a carrier uniform. Everyone who'd seen Carl confirmed that Hugh had, indeed, had a ghostly encounter.

Another postal employee, Marnie Willingham, was also startled by Carl's ghost.

One afternoon, she was in the Postmaster's office with the door closed. The Postmaster and Rick Hyde were assisting a customer at the window. There were only three employees in the office at the time.

Suddenly, a loud knock on the door scared Marnie so badly she screamed. She immediately looked through the window in the door but no one was there. Thinking the guys were playing a trick on her, she opened the door and went to the lobby where Hugh and Rick were still with a customer. They denied any pranks and the customer vouched for their presence at the window.

Marnie says that when she works alone in the office now, she leaves the door wide open.

After several unexpected encounters with Carl, two custodians actually refused to go to the basement to clean or procure supplies. Both eventually quit working at the Sheffield Post Office.

No one knows why Carl chooses to stay. Perhaps he has unfinished business he wishes to complete at the Sheffield Post Office.

In any case, he seems like a friendly spirit.

THE LADY SPIRIT OF COBY HALL

Coby Hall, at 459 North Court Street, in Florence, originally known as Courtland Mansion, was built in the 1830s, by John Simpson.

John Simpson

Simpson was born in County Tyrone, Ireland, on August 17, 1790. At the age of twenty-six, he was brought to Florence by James Jackson, builder of the Forks of Cypress, to buy land and operate a mercantile business. His store was on the corner of Alabama Street and Court Street and he became a very wealthy man from his land dealings and business.

In 1825, he returned to Ireland to marry his childhood sweetheart, Margaret Patton, (no relation to the Sweetwater Pattons). Margaret was born September 30, 1794, in Belfast.

When the newlyweds boarded the Tuscarora in Liverpool, Margaret was two months pregnant. The couple arrived in Philadelphia on New Year's Day, 1825. And then John brought his bride back to Florence where he began construction on a mansion between Court and Pine Streets in Florence.

Margaret Simpson became quite famous throughout Florence for her striking beauty.

The Simpsons loved to entertain and in 1839, they hosted a dance in the mansion.

One of the guests, a professor from LaGrange College named Dr. Harrington, became dangerously infatuated with Margaret and as they danced, he bragged to the other guests that she was *Mrs.* Harrington.

After the dance, Margaret's youngest brother, John, heard of Harrington's overtures and took it as a personal insult to his sister's honor. John spent the night searching Florence for Harrington and finally found him hiding out, ironically, in Simpson's store. John's intent was to thrash him to death with a horse whip. But Harrington, in a mix of self-defense and anger, drew his sword, which was concealed in the sheath of his walking stick, and slashed John to pieces, killing him in Simpson's store.

The body of young John lay in state for several days in the Courtland Mansion parlor until his burial in the Florence Cemetery.

It is believed the Simpson plot was the first in the Florence Cemetery.

The original Courtland Mansion burned in 1842, and was rebuilt to its present specifications in 1843.

John Simpson retired from his business in 1855. He and Margaret had seven sons and two daughters.

Isaac Patton Simpson drowned in nearby Cypress Creek on June

26, 1851.

And another son was killed at the Battle of Manassas during the Civil War. He is buried in the Florence Cemetery.

John Patton's gravestone, Florence Cemetery

Courtland Mansion / Irvine Place circa 1930

Though the home was occupied by both armies during the Civil War, it is believed that Confederate General John Bell Hood used the house as his headquarters before marching into Tennessee and the ill-fated battles of Franklin and Nashville.

Margaret Simpson died on August, 22, 1851, and John Simpson passed away December 13, 1865.

Margaret Simpson's grave, Florence Cemetery

In 1853, James Bennington Irvine, a wealthy planter, married Virginia Foster, daughter of George Washington Foster, who built

Courtview (now Rogers Hall). Foster presented the young couple with Mapleton, a lovely antebellum home which still stands on Pine Street, as a wedding gift. They did not live there long because Virginia thought the house was too far out of town - and they also believed it to be haunted.

Simpson plot, Florence Cemetery

To appease his daughter, Foster then bought Courtland Mansion in 1867. The name was changed to Irvine place.

James Irvine fought in the Civil War, was captured, and spent many months in prison at Johnson's Island on Lake Erie.

One interesting note about the Irvine family is that they were related to Washington Irving who penned *Sleepy Hollow*, the thrilling novel about the headless horseman.

While the Irvines lived in the home, it was occupied by both Federal and Confederate troops. When Confederate General John Bell Hood stopped in Florence to rendezvous with Nathan Bedford Forrest, he quartered in Irvine Place. Hood only had one arm and one leg, and his horse had to be brought to the front steps so his soldiers could literally strap him into the saddle.

Back of Courtland Mansion / Irvine Place circa 1930

The home was later inherited by Mrs. Madding King, the great granddaughter of Irvine. After World War II, the Kings restored the home to many of its present architectural features.

The solid brick house is situated on a spacious lawn, surrounded by magnolia, oak, and other trees. A walk, edged by ancient English boxwood, graces the approach from Court Street to the front porch which is bordered by square columns. A simple design was chosen for the house itself, which was influenced by the Federal period of architecture. The lines are straight and without ornament but the charm lies in the magnificent proportions of the structure. The basic floor plan consists of a spacious hall running through the house from the east entrance to the west entrance. Large solid walnut doors divide the double parlors downstairs.

Upon descending to the basement area, which served as a tea room in the 1990s, there is a long brick floored hall, first used as the dining room with four large rooms opening from it. The original kitchen was directly under the west parlor.

Italian marble mantles served as the focal points of the double parlors and when the Irvine family resided in the house, Ormolu candelabras, antique Regency mirrors, and Georgian crystal chandeliers adorned the parlors.

In 1981, then-owner, Ellis Coats, allowed Project Courtview to use the handsome mansion for Florence's first Decorators' Showhouse, as part of the fund-raising effort to restore Rogers Hall. Later, it became the corporate headquarters for Ed Robbins' Intervinyl Corporation.

In the early 1990's, David Brubaker purchased the home and

donated it to the University of North Alabama in memory of his deceased wife Coby Stockard Brubaker, who lost her bravely fought battle with cancer.

Today, Coby Hall hosts University functions, the UNA Alumni's annual Festival of Trees, and is available for community rental for events such as weddings, receptions, and dinners.

Courtland Manor is known as Coby Hall today, and is part of the University of North Alabama Campus

With such a rich history, Coby Hall must certainly have at least one restless soul within its solid brick walls.

The current employees are rarely bothered by disembodied spirits but on occasion, they have heard unexplainable noises and felt the unseen presence of another person in their midst.

One employee had gone to pour himself a cup of coffee when he heard footsteps come up behind him in the kitchen. But when he turned to speak to what he thought was a fellow co-worker, no one was there.

While eating lunch one day in one of the downstairs parlors, one lady who works in the building, saw a lady, dressed in a navy skirt and white blouse, pass through the foyer. Thinking someone was lost, the employee went to see if she could be of assistance, but the woman had vanished.

Karen Christian, who also is an employee of the Continuing Studies program, had an unexplainable - and unnerving - experience in the home as well. One evening, after locking up for the night, she was waiting on the front steps for her husband to come pick her up from work. Suddenly, the doorknobs began to rattle violently as if someone were trying to get out of the house. Thinking she had accidentally locked someone in, Karen unlocked the door and searched the house, finding no one inside.

One student worker had an experience which left him shaken. He had been carrying chairs down to the basement and setting them up for an event which was to be held in the tea room. As he reached the top of the stairs on his way back up for another load, he heard the grating of chairs on the brick floor in the basement.

He never liked to work in the house after hours following that incident.

Another man was passing through the foyer when he also glimpsed the lady in the navy skirt and white blouse in the downstairs parlor. When he backed up to see if she needed help, she was gone.

The clothes of the mysterious lady in the navy skirt are always described as modern. But who could she be?

No doubt she was a woman who dearly loved the house. She seems very comfortable with the earthly presences at Coby Hall and she only wants to make certain that the home continues the reputation of gracious living the mansion has always maintained.

THE COFFEE-REISMAN HOUSE HAUNTING

In the heart of the historic district, on one of Florence's oldest streets, stands a lovely Queen Anne style Victorian home, known as the Coffee-Reisman house. The 2 ½ story house at 618 North Wood Avenue with its combination of pyramidal and gabled roofs, weather board and shingled siding, L shaped porch and Eastlake trim, is one of the most beautiful Victorian houses in Florence. A finial piece tops a square tower on the front of the house. Intricate cornices trim the eaves. The high pitched gabled roof is supported by nine turned posts. Balusters and handrails connect the turned posts adding to the lacey woodwork which is representative of the elegant Victorian style.

The house was lovingly restored both inside and out by Benji Wilson and Bobbie Tomsik who lived there in the early 21st century with their children, Savannah and Drake.

The family also shared their home with several restless spirits. Who these spirits were in life is somewhat of a mystery since the Coffee-Reisman house has always been a place of historical significance and home to several families and boarders.

The house was built in the late 1880s, by Mark Reisman, one of the first Jewish merchants in the area. Mark and his wife, Hannah Reisman, purchased the land from William J. and Eugenia Wood for the sum of $1,500.

The Reismans owned a dry goods business in downtown Florence, on the corner of Court Street and Tennessee Street, where

Mefford's Jewelers now stands. One *Florence Herald* reporter stated that Reisman came to Florence around 1886, from Decatur, Alabama, and opened his store under the firm name of Reisman & Friedman. A *Florence Times* article reported that Reisman moved to Florence from Tuscaloosa. Hannah, was from Nashville. They had two children: A son named Emanuel and a daughter named Sadie Bell. The Reismans later changed the name of their business to *The Atlanta Store.*

This photograph of the Atlanta Store, on the corner of Court Street and Tennessee Street in Florence, was taken in the late nineteenth century.

Mark Reisman was a key player in getting the first Jewish temple in Florence built.

Outwardly, Mark Reisman seemed to be a prosperous merchant, family man, and model citizen. But on Saturday morning, October 5, 1901, Mark Reisman told his son, Emanuel, that he was going upstairs to clean his pistol. After a few moments, a shot was heard and Reisman was found on the floor outside his bedroom door with a bullet hole through his head.

His obituary was in both the *Florence Herald* and the *Florence Times.*

Florence Herald, Thursday Oct 10, 1901

Mark Reisman Dead.

Shot Through the Head with a Pistol:

Buried at Nashville.

The city was startled Saturday morning to learn of the tragic death of Mark Reisman, one of the oldest and best known merchants of Florence, which occurred at his home about 7 a.m. Reisman had told his son Manuel that he was going to clean his pistol. In a few minutes a report was heard and he was found on the floor with a bullet hole through his head. Death ensued a few minutes after the shot was fired. The remains were taken to Nashville Saturday night by the way of Stevenson, Ala., and the burial took place Sunday afternoon. Mr. Reisman came to the city fifteen years ago from Decatur and opened under the firm name of Reisman & Friedman. He had been a successful merchant and was liked by all who came in contact with him. Deceased leaves a wife and two children. The Messrs. Glick, of Nashville and Henderson, KY., are in the city and will look after the business of the deceased which is temporarily closed but will be opened in a few days.

The *Florence Times* report of Reisman's death, on Friday, October 11, 1901, was somewhat more detailed.

Mr. Reisman Dead.

Tragic Death of a Prominent Citizen.

Our Community Shocked at The Horrible Affair.

On Saturday morning last, between the hours of 7 and 8 o'clock, Mr. Mark Reisman, one of our most prominent merchants and most widely known citizens, met his death in a most tragic and horrible manner. He was shot through the head with a 38 caliber Smith and Wesson pistol, and after lingering less than an hour passed into eternity. He had arisen early to go to the store, and remarked that while waiting breakfast he would go upstairs and clean up his pistol. In a few moments the report of the pistol was heard and family rushed to the room and found him lying on the floor, with a wound through the head. The bullet had entered the right side of the head, a little above the ear, and had come out about the same position on the left side. He was removed from the floor to the bed, and within an hour expired. The family regards the shocking event as an accident.

The news of the dreadful event quickly spread through the city and many friends went to the stricken home to offer such assistance as they could. The community was profoundly shocked, and all day a gloom appeared to pervade the city.

On the midnight southern train the body, escorted to the depot by the Masonic fraternity and other friends, was carried by the stricken family, via Stevenson, to Nashville, where, at 2:30 o'clock Sunday, the interment took place.

In the death of Mr. Reisman our city has lost one of its leading citizens. Having been a leading merchant here for the past eighteen years, he was widely and familiarly known, and the news of his death was sad intelligence, indeed, to many friends both here and elsewhere.

The deceased came to Florence from Tuscaloosa about eighteen years ago, and since that time he was engaged tin the mercantile business, in which he was highly successful, and he leaves his family, a wife, and son and daughter, in very comfortable circumstances. He carried life insurance to the extent of $13,000.

Mr. Reisman was prominent in fraternal society circles, was a thorough business man, and was always interested in the public welfare. In his deplorable and untimely passing away he has left many friends sincerely grieved, who extend to the heart-broken family their profound sympathy.

The blood stain is still visible, a dark oval blotch soaked into the hardwood floor in the upstairs hall.

But whether Mark Reisman suffered an unfortunate accident or committed suicide is debatable.

Not long after the Bobbie and Benji moved into the house, Bobbie began to hear heavy footsteps pacing in the hall where

Reisman shot himself. After hearing this several times, and determining the noise was not being made by workmen, Bobbie called out to the spirit. The footsteps ceased at the sound of her voice.

Perhaps this is the restless spirit of Mark Reisman who undeniably died with unfinished business.

The Coffee-Reisman House, 618, N Wood Avenue, Florence

It is difficult to tell because several families have since called the Coffee-Reisman house, home.

On February 20, 1903, the house was purchased by Camilla Madding Jones Coffee for $5,350. Camilla's husband was Captain Alexander Donaldson Coffee, a son of one of the founders of Florence, General John Coffee.

A. D., as he was known, attended school in Florence and then in Nashville before returning to take charge as executor of Hickory Hill Place, the Coffee estate. He was a well-to-do cotton planter and was known throughout Florence as a well-read and prominent citizen.

The Coffees lived at Hickory Hill Place, but bought the lovely Victorian to use as a their town house.

Their only child, a daughter, Eliza Croom Coffee, for whom the municipal hospital in Florence was named, also lived in the house.

According to William McDonald's book, *The Story of Eliza Coffee Memorial Hospital*, not much is known about Eliza. She was born August 18, 1879, at the Ardoyne Plantation about four miles west of Florence on Gunwaleford Road. She was a quiet, studious and religious young lady who was known for her extraordinary beauty. Throughout most of her life, Eliza was frail and sickly.

She graduated from Florence Synodical College and was elected historian for the Florence Chapter of the United Daughters of the Confederacy. In fact, Florence and Lauderdale County Civil War history was her primary interest. She was also an accomplished pianist who participated in recitals at Brevard College near Ashville, North Carolina, where the Coffees owned a summer residence.

Eliza became ill early in 1904, either from an ulcer condition or malaria. When her ailment did not improve, Camilla took her to their summer cottage where she died on September 4, 1904, at the age of 25. Her body was brought back to Florence where she was buried in the Coffee family cemetery at Hickory Hill Place.

In memory of Eliza, Camilla gifted $10,000 for the building of a hospital. In 1919, she also donated the land behind the Reisman-Coffee house on which the first Coffee High School was built.

In 1941, the Maples family rented the home from the Coffee heirs. John Malcolm Maples was a doctor who converted a large downstairs closet into an examining room where he saw and treated patients. He and his wife, Irene Raney Maples, eventually purchased the home in 1952.

According to Ronald and Brenda Pettus, in their book, *History of Killen, Alabama - Once Known as Masonville*, Dr. Maples was born in Limestone County in 1872. He settled in the Killen / Center Star area around 1912. He lived in a large house located on Highway 72 which was destroyed around 1939, when his grandson accidentally set fire to it. Maples was a well-known and respected doctor. His practice was varied. He treated various illnesses and also delivered several babies.

After Dr. Maples died, his wife lived in the downstairs part of the house and rented the rooms upstairs. After her death in 1961, the house stood vacant until Elizabeth Maples Looft and her husband, Theodore, returned from Chicago in 1967. The Loofts lived in the house until the Wilson's bought it in the late 1990s.

None of the former owners ever admitted to feeling the presence of unearthly inhabitants in the house. Perhaps restoration efforts sparked the recent sightings and other paranormal occurrences in the house.

While the house was under restoration, one painter heard a woman's laughter come from right behind him. The experience so unnerved him, he didn't like to work in the house alone afterwards.

One morning, as Bobbie walked up the stairs, something caught her attention. She looked and, standing in the hallway in front of her daughter's room, was a little girl who appeared to be about eight years old. With shoulder length, brown hair pulled back with a ribbon and a high collared, ankle length, cream colored dress, the child stood and stared. Shocked by the child's appearance, Bobbie blinked and when she looked again, the little girl had vanished.

Benji was skeptical when Bobbie told him about the little girl. That is, until they had a party one night and WQLT DJ, Jimmy Oliver, walked in and asked who the little girl in the den was. Bobbie explained to him that there weren't any children in the house. Adamant that he had seen a child, he described the same little girl Bobbie had seen on the stairs. The family became convinced they were sharing their house with its former occupants.

Often, they would hear the unmistakable sound of a child walking in the upstairs hall or playing with toys in the children's rooms. Then two-year old, Drake Wilson, would point at an entity, only he could see, declaring, "There's that *goost*, Mommy. Sometimes, it comes in my room and gets my toys."

One evening in October, 2002, Bobbie and Benji were awakened during the night by the sound of a windup toy moving. Both children were sound asleep. Benji got up to investigate and when he walked into Drake's room, other toys began to wind up, seemingly of their own accord as if an unseen child were playing with them.

After separate incidents, Bobbie's mother, as well as Benji's, refused to housesit for the Wilsons. While the Wilsons were away, Benji's mother, Jan, decided to show the house to some friends. She took a lady up to the tower room on the third floor and suddenly all the lights switched off. Jan had the overwhelming feeling the spirits in the house thought she was an intruder and were trying to get her to leave. According to Jan, they were successful!

The occurrences prodded Bobbie into investigating the history of the house. And although she felt she'd made friends with the spirits there, some of what she discovered unnerved her.

Bobbie learned of a legend that had circulated in the Wood Avenue district for years. Apparently, three bodies had been buried underneath the floor of the cellar in the Coffee-Reisman house. The details of the clandestine burial were sketchy. But all agreed that there were, indeed, three bodies buried there.

The Wilsons were introduced to psychic detective, Jeanette McClure, Ph.D., who offered to come to the house.

Dr. McClure, who holds degrees in psychology and business, as well as a doctorate in hypnosis, does personal consultations and private readings. She has appeared on the Sci-Fi Channel's *Sightings*, and has worked nationwide with police and families of victims on murder and missing person cases.

Without any prior information about the history of the house she arrived and sat down in the living room. Her first impression, upon entering the house, was of a man who had medium to dark hair and was about six feet tall. She said he carried a cane for ornamentation and in his later life, looked somewhat like Mark Twain. She said she felt this man was a doctor and that he was standing in front of the mantle. "His name started with an M," she said. "I'm also getting the name *Emanuel* and *Martha*. Was there an *Elizabeth* who lived here?"

Bobbie confirmed the names. Emanuel was Reisman's son. And Elizabeth was, undoubtedly, Eliza Coffee.

Jeanette also picked up the spirit of a child in the house and described her as being under ten-years old and having died of an accident involving a horse.

In all, Jeanette got good feelings about the house and the spirits there.

However, the vibrations she got in the cellar were something altogether different.

Just under the kitchen, is a small root cellar with stone walls and a concrete floor. Jeanette confirmed that there were indeed bodies buried there and told the Wilsons she thought it was three men. One was a dirty, thin white man. Another was an African American, she thought was called Ol' Squire, and the other was a man in his 20s. She believed the men got caught either trying to steal something or doing something illegal.

Jeanette's impression was that the men were beaten and held in the cellar until their captives, thinking them dead, buried them alive right there underneath the house.

Overall, the Wilson family felt the spirits there were pleased with the restoration of the home. They rather enjoyed sharing their house with its former occupants and were not afraid when they heard footsteps crossing the hardwood floors and noticed cold drafts, even in the heat of summer.

No doubt, the spirits who remain in the Coffee-Reisman house appreciated the careful attention to historical detail in renovating the house. But who knows about the three allegedly buried under cellar floor?

SPOOKS IN THE NANCE HOME

Rogersville, Alabama is the oldest community in East Lauderdale County. It was founded in 1820, by John Rogers. Gradually, as more settlers moved into the area, water transportation was developed, roads were laid out, and the area prospered.

One of the early settlers was a man named Daniel Nance. In 1840, he constructed a plantation home on Lambs Ferry Road in Rogersville. All the framework was put together with pegs and the house was trimmed with hand dressed lumber. The mansion, completed in 1844, had thick plaster walls and a wide stairway leading to the second floor.

The Nance home was a typical plantation home and attracted little unusual attention - until after the Civil War when it developed a reputation for being haunted.

During the war, a Confederate soldier stopped by the Nance well for a drink. Exhausted and thirsty, he turned the crank which drew up a weathered old wooden bucket. A dented dipper hung on a wood post nearby. He plunged it into the bucket and then lifted the dipper to his lips, propping his worn, muddy boot on the limestone curbing as he drank. After draining the dipper, he leaned back toward the bucket to refill it, inadvertently slumping against his gun. With a blast, the gun went off, mortally wounding the soldier.

The noise alerted the Nance family and they rushed the soldier into the Nance home. As he was helped up the stairs, his blood dripped onto the steps where it dried.

The soldier died in an upstairs bedroom near the fireplace - but the bloodstains remained on the stairway, despite many attempts to remove them.

The Nance Home in Rogersville

Mrs. B. R. Thornton, who had visited the home several times, claimed that Liza Nance, who lived in the home for many years, had shown her the bloodstains.

After the Civil War, the Nance family was forced to sell off portions of their plantation to meet the high Reconstruction era taxes, and the home fell into bad disrepair. By the early 1900's, most of the land had been sold and only three members of the Nance family, Molly, Liza, and Bob, lived in the house. None of them ever married and they kept to themselves.

Jesse King recounted a story of the ghost who lived in the house that often followed passersby home after dark. And one night, according to Mr. King, the ghost pursued a man for some distance and then broke his neck.

In reality, Bob Nance, the only surviving Nance male, did die from a broken neck when he fell from a tree while hunting.

Molly Nance died in the early 1940's. After this, Liza Nance shut herself up in the home and became a virtual recluse. She maintained that several ghosts lived in the house with her, claiming they rattled chains at night.

Every night, Liza would nail the doors and windows shut and refuse to let anyone in after dark. She closed off the rest of the house and moved into one downstairs room in the house, refusing to accept help from her friends and neighbors.

Gertrude Watkins, who sometimes worked for her, said Liza would sit before the fireplace, throwing cash into the fire, mumbling that she was burning her money to keep the ghosts from getting it. A woman who wished to remain anonymous recalled a childhood visit to the Nance home and vividly remembered Miss Nance pointing out the still visible bloodstains left by the dead soldier.

One night after nailing herself in, Miss Liza froze to death.

Neighbors, who stopped by the next day to check on her, noticed the house still boarded and broke in, discovering Liza Nance's corpse lying by a cold stove in freezing weather.

Attempts to revive her were unsuccessful.

The Nance home was torn down sometime afterward. But people who remember the ghost stories associated with the property, still look over their shoulders as they pass by the place with the Nance home once stood.

THE PICKETT PLACE POLTERGEIST

FLORENCE HAS SPOOKS states a Friday, February 22, 1907, article for *The Leighton News.*

Intelligent People Claim They Saw Them in an Old House

FLORENCE, Feb 17. - *Florence spiritualists are agog, while the more materialistic are scoffing over strange sights and sounds which are said to be seen and heard at an old place in the northern part of the city.*

The house is the old Crow place and for weeks, hundreds have visited the place, including all the local spiritualists. Among the latter it is believed that the house is the nightly stalking ground of ghostly visitors. Three having been plainly seen. At first, strange noises were heard which the family occupying the house were unable to account for, and a medium was called in. Sometime during the night the medium was awakened by cries and groans and following the sounds, came upon a soldier in gray whipping a slave. Another saw a white man in his shirt sleeves wearing a diamond stud and upon another occasion while a member of the family was at the telephone, a woman in black glided noiselessly through the hall.

The first noises occurred several weeks ago while the family were at supper and the sound was similar to that made by rapping on a boiler. It was repeated at irregular intervals in different parts of the room and it is in the dining room that most of the alleged apparitions have appeared.

The house is one of the oldest in Florence and is partly two stories while the remainder has an attic that is inaccessible. There are stories told of a slave being whipped to death in the old house many years ago, before it came in the possession of Major Crow, but this incident had long been forgotten and was only recalled after the appearance of the strange apparition. The spooks have not been seen by one person alone in most cases, but by as many as fourteen gathered in the dining room at one time.

While not believing in ghosts themselves, L.D. Buchanan and family, who occupied the house, were made so nervous by noises they could not explain that they moved out and new tenants are now in possession.

Pickett Place, Florence, Alabama

One of Florence's oldest houses, now known as Pickett Place, at 438 North Seminary Street, was built in 1833, by Thomas J. Crow as a wedding present for his new bride, Elizabeth Hooks of Tennessee.

The house was made of solid brick, faced with stucco, and originally looked much like Pope's Tavern before a second story was added. The basic floor plan consisted of a central hall with two rooms on either side of the first floor.

Crow had come to Florence from Kentucky in 1821, and had some connection with Andrew Jackson, who was a guest in the home.

The Crows' ancestors fled Scotland during the reign of James I and James II of England because of religious persecution.

Elizabeth gave birth to a son, James McCollough Crow, on March 16, 1836. He was educated in the Florence schools. At the outbreak of the Civil War, he was working as a book keeper for Rice Brothers. He fought gallantly during the war and was promoted to the rank of major. He was wounded at Richmond while serving with the Ninth Alabama from 1861, to Appomattox.

After the war, James M. Crow engaged in the dry goods business, but later got into the steamboat industry. In 1884, he was made Deputy United States Marshall and headquartered in Birmingham.

He also owned and operated the Florence Hotel.

In 1867, he married Mary Brandon and they had two children.

The Crows eventually moved to Jasper, Alabama, where they are buried. Mary died in 1878.

In 1886, a man named Richard Orick Pickett purchased the house. Pickett was the son of Steptoe and Sarah O. Chilton Pickett. He was born in Fauquier County, Virginia, August 22, 1823.

The Pickett family came to Alabama in 1829, and settled in Limestone County.

At the age of twenty, Richard Orik Pickett married Fannie Boggs. Soon afterward, he began to study law under James Irvine in Florence, was admitted to the bar in 1845, and began to practice law in Moulton where he represented Lawrence County in the legislature in 1849. He was also an elected judge in Lawrence County. In 1856, he was elected to represent the sixth congressional district of Alabama under President James Buchanan. He remained in Moulton until the outbreak of the Civil War.

Pickett raised a company of soldiers from Lawrence County that became known as Company H of the Thirty-fifth Alabama infantry. He entered the cavalry service and in November, 1863, was commissioned colonel of the Tenth Alabama cavalry under General Phillip Roddy's command.

Too ill to make the retreat, Colonel Pickett was captured upon the evacuation of Corinth. He was held until the following September when he was exchanged at Vicksburg.

At the end of the war, he returned to Moulton and resumed his law practice.

Pickett Place, Florence

In December, 1867, Pickett and his family moved to Florence.

In 1875, he served as a member of the constitutional convention from Lauderdale County. He also served in the legislature during the sessions of 1884-85, and 1886-87. Very active in politics, he was a delegate to the national convention that nominated Horatio Seymour for the presidency. He was also a delegate to the national convention that met in Chicago in 1884, which nominated Grover Cleveland for president.

The Picketts did not purchase Pickett Place until 1886. Of their nine children, only three daughters survived until maturity. One married Charles Patton, son of Alabama Governor Robert Miller Patton of Sweetwater Mansion.

Pickett served Florence as a judge and alderman. He and another alderman, Carl Dice, had an altercation involving the city trees. Dice advocated the removal of all street trees in the city and was heard to say, "Who ever heard of a growing western town with shade trees?"

One morning, Pickett discovered workmen at his gate with axes about to cut down his trees. Pickett raised an argument that "turned the air blue." But his trees remained untouched.

The house was used as an office by Dr. John B. Rice and Dr. Quintus Langstaff for forty years.

Dr. Timothy Ashley also had offices in Pickett Place.

In the late 1990s, the Bailey family purchased and restored the home to be used as a tea room and antique shop. It now serves as an event venue.

The dwelling has been rich with history and activity. Those who have occupied the house in more recent years, were surprised by the *Leighton News* article. Dr. Rice claimed that he never had any preternatural experiences while he owned the house, and Gina Bailey, who is the present owner, laughingly says she just doesn't want to know if there are spooks in the house.

Other employees have experienced things in the house they cannot explain. Inexplicable drafts. Footsteps when no one else is present, and indiscernible whispering.

Still, something must have happened in the house for a local newspaper to have covered the event in 1907. If the story about the slave being whipped to death on the stairs is true, it would have most likely occurred either during Crow's ownership of the home or while it was under construction. Undoubtedly, slave labor was used to build the house. Perhaps a servant was, indeed, beaten to death by a cruel overseer. It is interesting to note that Crow was a leading member of the Methodist Church but suddenly stopped attending church services.

The man in shirt sleeves who wore a diamond stud sounds much like Colonel Pickett who had acquired wealth as a lawyer.

But who was the woman in black? Perhaps she was a widow of one of the former owners.

The Evans family, who lived in the home for many years, claimed that gold had been buried in the basement, a common practice during the Civil War and Reconstruction period. Perhaps the spirits there are guarding buried treasure.

Whatever the case, the ghostly inhabitants do not seem to interfere with guests at events hosted in the lovely, historic home.

THE SPIRITS OF SWEETWATER MANSION

In 1828, a man named John Brahan moved to the Florence area and began construction on a home near a rushing creek. The Indian name for the creek was Succatania, which meant Sweetwater. Brahan thought the name suited the area, and dubbed his plantation Sweetwater. Many local folks know it as the Weeden home today.

John Brahan

The house was made of clay brick which was made in cypress molds and a kiln on the property.

But the mansion had only been built as high up as the window sills when John Brahan suddenly became sick and died. His body was buried in the woods near the unfinished house. His grave is marked with an upside down torch, 19th century funerary art which signifies *a life extinguished*, meaning that he left this life too soon.

The house came into the hands of Robert Patton who was a politician as well as a merchant and planter. He served in both the House and the Senate of the Alabama Legislature for several years until he was elected Governor in 1865. He completed the construction of Sweetwater, following Brahan's plans.

Robert Miller Patton

Four large rooms divided by a central hall graced the first floor. The two on the left were large reception rooms separated by soaring folding doors. The bedrooms occupied the East side of the house. Spacious upstairs rooms were used as bedrooms for the children and guests.

A brick out-building served as a kitchen, weaving room, and icehouse. Ice was cut from the creek during hard winter freezes and stored in the deep well under the icehouse.

The basement housed several rooms which were used as a wine cellar, a pantry, and a laundry room. There is also one room which can be seen from a small window, but mysteriously no doors to permit an entrance.

The Pattons and their descendants made Sweetwater their home for almost 140 years.

Three Patton boys served in the Confederate Army during the Civil War. And this is where our ghost story starts.

A slave at Sweetwater named Sam went away with the Confederate Army to be with his young master, Billy Patton. Sam and Billy, who were only a year apart in age, had grown up together.

Billy Patton

During the charge at Shiloh, Billy Patton was killed instantly when a shot struck him in the forehead. Sam had to wait until the fighting was over at dusk so he could retrieve the body. He placed the corpse in a small log hut which was being used for a sutler's store and then walked back over the dark battleground to the camp.

The Confederates were forced to retreat to Corinth the next day but Sam refused to leave the field with the retreating army. During the night, he found the sutler's hut and recovered Billy's body. Sam then found the body and carried it to Corinth. From there, he brought Billy back to Florence, across the Tennessee River and through the front gate of the Sweetwater Plantation.

Sweetwater Mansion 1930s

Since that time, caretakers at Sweetwater have heard the sounds of women crying and sniffing, of skirts swishing across the hard wood floor, coming from the foyer. Upon investigation, Billy Patton's entire funeral can be viewed. The coffin is placed in the foyer between the West rooms and two large torch like candles stand vigil beside it. Patton family members, dressed in black, view the body which is clad in a Confederate uniform.

Hall where Billy Patton lay in state

Note the ghostly figure in the center of the room

One caretaker related this story to Florence City Historian, William McDonald, and he confirmed the details of Billy Patton's funeral which he had learned from historical research.

Another ghost story associated with Sweetwater also comes from the Civil War era. When General Sherman came to Florence, one of his divisions made camp at Sweetwater. They raided the house early on and took all the meat and provisions, including the contents of the wine cellar. Horses and cows were confiscated along with the Patton family valuables. The slave cabins on the grounds were used as infirmaries for soldiers suffering from a smallpox epidemic. Two of the cabins were used to cremate the bodies of the victims.

At least one clerk from the convenience store near the property has seen the spirit of one of the slaves. Dressed in a pair of tattered trousers, he solemnly walks by, staring and shaking his head despondently.

Parties can be heard taking place in the front reception room. The piano plays at night and if the lid and fallboard are closed, they will be found reopened in days.

One of Sweetwater Mansion's double parlors, 1930s

Once, one caretaker saw a woman standing on the stairs, brushing her long hair. Presumably the woman's spirit enjoys looking at her reflection in mirrors. One evening, the door to the caretaker's quarters opened of its own accord. The caretaker's dogs immediately began to snarl and bark at the unseen entity. When the caretaker looked up to see what was going on, a broken shard of mirror floated off the mantle and into the air as if someone were examining their reflection. The caretaker demanded that the spirit show itself. Then, the mirror sailed back onto the mantle and the door closed abruptly behind a sudden gust of cold air.

Apparently, the slave cemetery was at the corner of Weeden school and the school itself is home to a friendly spirit or two. Toilets flush on their own and footsteps can be heard in the empty hallways at night.

One of Sweetwater Mansion's bedrooms

Though recent efforts were made to save the mansion, Sweetwater, today, is sadly in bad disrepair. The once immaculate grounds are grown up and the grand porches on the house have long since fallen in.

The mansion is not open for tours or visitors and the *No Trespassing* signs are very strictly enforced.

Sweetwater Mansion, circa 2002

VIOLET

Ghosts are not always frightening, see-through apparitions that appear standing at the foot of your bed in the middle of a stormy night. Sometimes, they are as solid as you and I. But that does not make them any less terrifying.

Geneva Yerbey has never seen such a ghost. But her brother has.

The experience so frightened him, he still does not like to recount his story. In fact, he was so shaken by the strange events, he refuses to return to the little country cemetery where the incident took place.

On a Saturday night in the early 1960s, "John" dropped his girlfriend off at her house which was just across the state line in Tennessee. He pulled out of the driveway and started back home. As he drove, the light drizzling rain started to come down harder. He flipped on the wipers and instinctively slowed down, recalling what his father had told him about the roads being slick when it first started to rain. Besides, Savannah Highway was a dangerous road at night. Several people had lost their lives navigating the sharp twists and turns on the old narrow road.

In the glare of the headlights, he noticed something up ahead. As he got closer, he saw it was a girl wearing a thin summer dress and walking alone down the side of the dark road.

John slowed down, wondering if she'd gotten into a fight with her boyfriend and then put out on the side of the road. Something in his gut told him to stop the car. He reached across the seat and rolled down the window. "Hey, need a lift?"

She turned and tucked a strand of her light brown hair behind her ear. "Yeah. Thanks for stopping," she said and scooted into the front seat beside him. She shivered and hugged her arms to herself.

"Here, you're cold," he said and shirked off his jacket. He handed it to her. "Where are you headed?"

"Thanks." She slipped the jacket on. "I'm going to my mother's house. It's just a couple of miles down the road."

John shifted into first and pulled back out onto the highway. An awkward silence fell over them but John didn't try to make conversation. The girl looked upset and he guessed she was probably embarrassed about being dumped on the side of the road. Guys could be such jerks sometimes.

The girl pointed at a dirt road up ahead. "Turn there."

John followed the dirt road to an old farmhouse.

"This is the place," the girl said, her voice soft and faraway.

John pulled into a washed out dirt driveway. "I'm John. What's your name?"

She stepped out of the car. "Violet," she said and gave him a demure smile. "Thanks for the lift."

"No problem," he said and watched her walk toward the house for a while before he drove off.

A few miles down the road, he realized she still had his jacket and decided he'd just pick it up the next week when he was back up that way.

The following Saturday, he stopped at Violet's house on the way to pick up his girlfriend. In the daylight, the old house looked abandoned and he wondered, at first, if he'd remembered the way here correctly. The porch and roof sagged and the dull white paint had seen better days. However, smoke drifted up out of the crumbling chimney, so John hopped out of his car and walked across the neglected yard and up onto the porch.

The front door creaked open and a woman peeked through the crack which was secured by a chain lock. "Who are you?" she demanded.

"My name's John. Is Violet home?"

The door closed abruptly and John heard the chain rattling as the woman unlocked the door and then swung it wide open. "Did you know my Violet?"

"Well, sort of. I gave her a ride home last Saturday and let her borrow my jacket. I just stopped by to pick it up."

The lady's wrinkled forehead furrowed. "You must be mistaken."

"No. This is where I dropped her off."

The woman's face darkened. "Violet has been dead for ten years. She was killed in a car wreck just a few miles down the road."

"But I . . . I dropped her off here just last week."

Tears welled in her pale blue eyes. "We buried her in the cemetery up the road." With that, she slammed the door.

John heard the chain rattle as she slid the lock back into place.

Bewildered, he walked back to his car. Why would that lady tell him Violet had been dead ten years? Did they just want to keep his coat? He sighed and headed back toward Savannah Highway to pick up his girlfriend.

On the way, he passed by the cemetery. Curious, he parked the car and got out. "This is silly," he said aloud to himself but a cold chill swept up his spine just the same.

And then he saw it - his mud spattered coat draped over a cold marble tombstone.

John's breath froze in his chest as he neared the grave. His knees threatened to give way and he swallowed the lump of trepidation in his throat. With one quick movement, he snatched the coat off the headstone, his heart skipping a beat when he saw the name etched in the marble.

Violet. . . .

THE GHOSTS OF WOODLAWN PLANTATION

The early settlers of North Alabama were, for the most part, of Scotch-Irish descent. The pioneers of old Florence read, traveled, and were the first entrepreneurs in a time when the Shoals area was considered wilderness.

One of these early settlers was a man named James Hood from Cascum, County Downe, Ireland. He came to America prior to 1800, and settled first in Philadelphia. He received American citizenship December 9, 1803.

Through contacts in Nashville, Tennessee, he became friends and business partners with fellow Irishman, James Jackson, of the Forks of Cypress.

Hood purchased a plantation and settled in St. Mary's Parrish near New Orleans, Louisiana, but the climate did not agree with his health and he moved to Lauderdale County where his friend, Jackson, lived. No doubt, James Jackson praised the Shoals area's beautiful countryside, abundant creeks, and prime farming land to Hood.

James Hood made his first purchase of lands about 3 miles west of Florence, in Lauderdale County, on March 4th, 1818. He continued to buy land surrounding his property and elsewhere in Alabama until his death in 1839.

He hired Nathaniel H. Marks to construct a log cabin on the property on October 20, 1819. He also contracted him for a brick home which was to be built in the future.

That same year, Hood married Mary Ann Chalmers of Newton Stewart, Scotland. He referred to Mary as his "wee bonny Scotch bride" and he brought her back to Florence to live in the newly built log cabin. It was Mary Hood who drew the design for the "big house" as a replica of the home she'd left behind in Scotland.

The plantation contained over 2000 acres at the time and was known first as Hoodlawn and later, Woodland. Over time, the name changed to Woodlawn Plantation and is known by that title today.

Woodlawn Plantation

Mary took special delight in duplicating the fanlight over the front doorway. Slaves set to work making brick from the native red clay. The house was not completed until 1832, over ten years after construction was begun. Each brick was hand laid by slaves. Both the interior and exterior walls of the house are four bricks thick.

The house itself, is of the Federal style, a two-story brick mansion with a double entrance and twenty-four paned windows. A long veranda, complete with Ionic columns, stretches the length of the back.

Slaves skilled in woodworking, hand carved the mantels and other woodwork in the home. Boxwood shrubs were planted to border the walkway from the circular driveway to the wide stone steps. The steps were known throughout the county for their gleaming whiteness. Each day, slaves scrubbed the soft stone until it shone.

The wide, hospitable doorway opens onto a center hall which is graced by a stairway.

Woodlawn, circa 1930

Not long after Woodlawn was completed, on the night of

November 12, 1833, a meteor shower rained down on the Alabama countryside. Panic stricken, the servants gathered in the backyard fearing it was the end of times. Mary Ann Hood stood on the back gallery and read aloud passage after passage from the Bible. Still, there were some too frightened to be calmed. After James Hood cajoled and attempted to explain what was happening to the inconsolable slaves, he finally resorted to vocabulary colorful enough to calm them.

"It mustn't be too bad," one was heard to mutter. "If the master thought he was goin' to die, he sure wouldn't be talkin' like that!"

Woodlawn, circa 1930

That meteor storm was described as one of the most intense in recorded history. Its memory seemed to stick with Alabamians long after it was forgotten elsewhere. *The Florence Gazette* reported, *"thousands of luminous bodies, shooting across the firmament in every direction. There was little wind and not a trace of clouds, and the meteors succeeded each other in quick succession producing a remarkable scene of natural grandeur, which may be more readily conceived than described."*

Later in the nineteenth century, historian, R.M. Devens listed the display as one of the hundred most memorable events in American history.

Little was known about meteor storms and their source in 1833. Those who did not attribute the spectacle to supernatural causes probably blamed the weather. No doubt, more than a handful of gamblers, thieves, and other assorted sinners in the south, repented that night.

One of the Woodlawn slaves, a woman named Hattie, married a slave called Parson Dick, who served as a groom, from the nearby Forks of Cypress plantation. The wedding took place in the kitchen, and although the two slaves were married, they never lived together as man and wife.

Parson Dick continued to be held by the Jackson family and Hattie remained in the service of the Hoods.

The Jacksons loved Parson Dick and he, apparently, was fond of them as well. James Jackson purchased him in New Orleans because he was an excellent groom. Since Jackson raised and raced thoroughbred horses, he wanted someone of great intelligence and patience to attend his racehorses. The Jacksons were known to have treated Parson Dick as one of the family and after James Jackson died in the 1840s, Parson Dick became Mrs. Jackson's valet.

He established a church for the slaves at the Forks of Cypress. Apparently, his congregation got into the spirit. Complaints were made about all the noise coming from the church, so Parson Dick placed upside down wash pots on the floor to reduce the noise.

When the famous horse painter, Edmund Troy came to the Forks of Cypress to paint Jackson's prize winning horses, Peytona and Glencoe, he became fascinated by Parson Dick's unusual appearance and asked if the Jacksons would mind if he painted his portrait. The Jacksons agreed and they displayed the portrait in the hall at the Forks of Cypress until after Mrs. Jackson's death.

Portrait of Parson Dick

Sometime during the Civil war, Parson Dick left the Forks to visit Hattie at Woodlawn. He mysteriously disappeared and was never seen or heard from again. No trace of him was ever found. Everyone who knew Parson Dick believed he'd met with foul play. He was a devoted husband and father and would never have left of his own accord without his family. Some suspected he'd been abducted and forced into service by the Yankees.

After the Civil War, his portrait was given to relatives and also disappeared. In the late 80s or early 90s, some Jackson relatives were visiting a historic mansion at Williamsburg, Virginia and recognized the portrait. As it turned out, one of the Jackson descendants had married a Rockefeller. The Rockefellers were instrumental in funding the restoration of Williamsburg and the portrait had been donated to one of the historic buildings there.

The Jackson family procured the portrait and it hung in the Regions Bank of Florence, which is a close replica of the Forks of Cypress mansion, until Curtis Flowers, a Jackson descendant, pushed to have the portrait displayed in the Pope's Tavern Museum in Florence, where it hangs to this day.

Woodlawn in the 1930s

Mary Ann Hood was known throughout North Alabama as a woman of unusual charm and character who had a marked intellect and extraordinary business ability. She believed that one should have social as well as other duties and managed the estate after the death of her husband. She entertained and also traveled, not only in America, but made several trips back to Scotland during her lifetime.

At the onset of the Civil War, Mary Ann took her young grandsons to Scotland and enrolled them in the University of Edinburgh.

After the war, she returned and deeded farms to all her former slaves.

When her son, John Murray Hood, married Mary Cornelia Heslep in 1853, Mary Ann moved to Florence and left the Hood home to be carried on by the young couple.

Cornelia was the granddaughter of one of Alabama's earliest pioneers, Lewis B. Allen. Allen was related to Meriwether Lewis of the Lewis and Clarke Expedition.

In 1861, John Murray Hood sold the plantation to Martin, Weakley & Company. He and his family moved to Tunica County, Mississippi. Martin, Weakley & Co. owned and operated three large cotton mills on Cypress Creek. Two of these mills were burned during the Civil War. The last ceased operations in the early twentieth century.

During the Civil War, the Woodlawn plantation was used as a camp ground for both Federal and Confederate troops. Confederate General, Nathan Bedford Forrest's troops quartered on the grounds. The house itself was used as a headquarters. The Federal troops camped all around the house and burned the furniture for firewood. Supposedly, there is a soldier buried near the front gate.

Alex Coffee, who was associated with Martin and Weakley, purchased Woodlawn and lived there nine years. John Hood and his family returned to Alabama after the Civil War and in 1869, he bought the house back and a portion of the plantation. He moved back into it in January, 1870.

John and Cornelia had nine children before John's untimely death and once more, a woman was left at the helm of Woodlawn.

Woodlawn was later left to John and Cornelia's son, Alabama's first Admiral, Admiral John Hood, one of the survivors of the U.S.S. Maine, which exploded in Havana Harbor. He fought in the Battle of Santiago and during WWI, was responsible for the laying of the Pacific Cable.

Admiral Hood died at Woodlawn in 1919. After his death, his wife moved to Florence and left the "big house" at Woodlawn to be used as a barn. Hay was stored upstairs and livestock was boarded downstairs.

A present descendant of the Hood family is Mrs. Tom Heflin.

Woodlawn was saved by Dr. Shaler S. and Minnie Roberts who bought the run down mansion in 1929, to restore and preserve it. Shaler Roberts Jr. remembered seeing the house before the restoration. Sheets of tin had been placed over the windows. Cotton was baled and stored in several rooms. Mules were stabled in one of the rooms. Peas and other vegetables were stashed in the house. The original log cabins and slave quarters deteriorated and fell in while the Roberts owned the property.

Mrs. Roberts traveled the south and purchased period antiques for the home. Dr. Roberts raised and showed Tennessee Walking Horses. He also had an avid interest in fox hunting and kept a kennel of fox hounds.

Shaler Roberts Jr. also remembered hearing the tale of one of General Nathan Bedford Forrest's soldiers who was buried near the gates. He said that as a child he searched for the grave but was never able to locate it. He did find several old bullets and a broken bayonet on the property.

He slept in the room where Admiral Hood died but said he was never bothered by any ghost there.

Hank and Laura Jane Self purchased Woodlawn in 1985, and continued the restoration, paying special detail to historical accuracy.

The present owners purchased the house from the Selfs and, like the families before them, enjoy living in historic Woodlawn. However, the property came with a little more than they bargained for.

It's no wonder that a place so rich in history is home to several restless spirits.

Several people who've lived in the house have reported hearing the sound of a baby crying coming from the woods. One lady who lived there, heard a voice calling, "Momma," and became so frightened she called the home where her own children were attending a spend-the-night party, requesting that the hosts check on her children and confirm they were there safely asleep in the bed.

A search of the woods turned up nothing or no one - no one that could be seen, anyway.

Mysterious banging sounds have been heard all over the house.

A house sitter for the present owner was awakened in the night by a friend who heard him talking in his sleep. When he asked, "Who are you talking to?" The house sitter said, "The people camped in the yard."

One night, the present owners were staying at their lake camp when their alarm company called and reported that the alarm had been set off. They drove to Woodlawn. The alarm was still sounding but the house seemed secure. No doors or windows had been broken into. When they went inside and flipped the light switch, however, nothing happened. The house was in complete darkness. As they walked into the foyer, they heard the shuffling of feet in the living room. The owner described it as sounding like more than one person. Afraid, they quickly checked the breaker box and discovered that the main switch had been thrown. When the lights came on, no one was found in the house.

The coffee maker has been known to come on by itself.

Different scents occasionally pervade the air. The sweet fragrance of flowers wafts through the master bedroom and the pungent odor of rubbing alcohol sometimes fills the room that was once used by Dr. Roberts as a bedroom. Often, the owners detect the smell of damp woolen fabric mingled with the woody scent of a campfire.

Woodlawn is fraught with cold spots and drafts that are especially noticeable on the stairs.

The indoor motion detectors go off, seemingly, for no reason.

One brick mason who was working alone heard footsteps behind him but when he turned to look, no one was there.

The owner was once passing by the dining room and out of the corner of her eye, saw, what she could only describe as, an overlay of people in long dresses and antiquated clothing apparently having a party of some sort.

The dogs often become alert and bark at unseen presences.

Former owners have reported seeing a man dressed in Civil War uniform standing in the meadow outside.

With all the activity Woodlawn has experienced in its two-hundred-year history, it is difficult to say who the spirits might be who still walk the high ceilinged rooms and grounds of the mansion.

Conceivably, the soldier in the meadow is the man who was supposedly buried at the gates. Rumors abound that the slave cemetery was plowed under for cotton planting. Could these spirits be haunting the home?

Is Mary Ann Hood still placing fresh flowers in her bedroom and entertaining in the dining room on some other level of existence? Perhaps Union and Confederate soldiers are still camping on the grounds on a plane of reality we only see and hear glimpses of.

The present owners are merely curious and don't really mind sharing their home with its former occupants. "After all," said the current owner, "they were there first."

THE HOLLERIN' THANG

Gilbert's father had given him a .38 Special Wesson revolver and he took comfort in its weight against his thigh. It was late. Too late. And too dark. Bessie was going to be mad, he thought. He chuckled to himself. She'd be mad alright, until she saw the twenty-five dollars he'd won. Since the stock market crash the year before in 1929, twenty-five dollars was right hard to come by.

Gilbert's horse plodded along by the faint light of the moon. He still had a long way to go and he muttered an oath at himself for playing that last hand – twenty-five dollars or not.

He guided the horse down toward the old wagon crossing across a slough backed up by the Tennessee River. The horse picked its way through the rocks and muddy water.

Gilbert was grateful the horse knew the way. It was so dark, he could hardly see anything at all.

A splash in the water suddenly caught his attention and he jerked his head in the direction of the noise. The horse came to a dead stop and Gilbert had to fight to control it.

"Who's there?" he called, squinting into the darkness.

And then he saw it.

He'd heard about it his entire life. He'd heard its unearthly screams coming out of the woods in the night. But he'd never seen it.

Until now.

Even in the darkness, it glowed, solid white, as big as a full grown man, with long snowy hair and eyes that glittered red in the moonlight.

The Hollerin' Thang.

Gilbert swallowed hard and spurred his horse into action. "Make tracks, horse!" he yelled and dug his heels in harder.

The spooked animal's hooves churned on the gravel.

But the Hollerin' Thang kept up, running right alongside Gilbert's horse. Gilbert drew his pistol and fired off two shots. He missed. And the Hollerin' Thang kept its wild pace, leaping over the ground as if it were almost flying.

Gilbert leaned down in his saddle and fired again, not stopping until he'd unloaded it. At least two of the shots hit the Hollerin' Thang but, undaunted, the creature continued to chase him.

The wild ride continued until they came to a fork in the road. The Hollerin' Thang veered off and ran down a logging road, disappearing into the night. Gilbert rode, hell bent for leather, straight home. When he arrived at his house, he didn't stop the horse until he got to the front porch. He leapt off and ran, breathless, into the house, leaving the poor horse to fend for itself. "Bessie Mae!" he yelled and snatched his shotgun off the rack in the hall. "Lock the door. The white thing was after me and I couldn't kill it!"

Throughout the years, as far back as anybody in the Harmony community can remember, stories and sightings of the Hollerin' Thang have circulated. It's been called The White Thing and also Slough Thing. But nearly everyone in the little community between Moulton and Town Creek has heard the ungodly screams stretching across the moon-bathed fields at night.

Gilbert's wife, Bessie, claimed she never needed an alarm clock when they lived on Old Bethel Mountain. The Hollerin' Thang's ungodly screams awakened her every morning at 5 a.m.

Gilbert was unfortunate enough to have a second encounter with the Hollerin' Thang in the 1960s.

As he lay dying of cancer, the terrifying sound of shrill shrieks came through his open window. But this time, he knew what the

Hollerin' Thang had come for. Often, when a person was ill, the Thang came and howled outside the window, an unnerving harbinger of death.

"Go on, now, Hollerin' Thang," he said, his voice weak from the ravaging cancer. "I'll be on down in a few days."

Gilbert's son, John, also heard the Hollerin' Thang late one night in the late 1960s, from the trailer on County Road 151, where he lived at the time.

His dogs started raising such a commotion, John looked out the window to see if something had come up in the yard. Suddenly, the dogs started whimpering and he heard them crawl under the trailer. They'd never acted like this before.

John peered out the window, the full moon casting an eerie glow across the deserted Terry Club and the steep bluff beyond. He stared. Something white leapt out of the woods, stopped and stared at him, and then scampered back into the trees once more.

Could it be the Hollerin' Thang? He'd heard the stories his father had told. Was this the creature who'd been haunting these sloughs and woods for nearly a century?

Shaken, he went back to bed. But he didn't sleep that night.

A woman named Shayla had an encounter in the early 60s, as well. One night, she was in her trailer on Loosier Road when she heard a noise that sounded like a woman screaming. Thinking someone was in trouble, she ran outside only to come face to face with the Hollerin' Thang.

She barely caught a glimpse of a tall creature, with long white hair, before it jumped, sailing over the top of the trailer. Shayla ran back inside and didn't go out until the next day. What she discovered, left her shaken.

Tangled in the barbed wire fence behind her trailer were several long white hairs.

Recent stories of the Hollerin' Thang are rare. But one man, Todd Bradford, had an encounter with it in 1983, when he was about thirteen-years old.

He was riding his four wheeler from Hatton on Cave Springs Road when he heard a noise that sounded like a horse whinnying in distress. The noise was shrill, bloodcurdling, and louder than any horse he'd ever heard. Todd looked to see what was causing such an unearthly sound.

Running alongside him, in broad daylight, was a very tall creature, which Todd said resembled Bigfoot or the Abominable Snowman. It stood on hind legs like a man and moved across the ground with long leaping motions. Todd had heard stories about the Hollerin' Thang all his life and he knew exactly what it was when he saw it.

His own grandmother had heard its screams. His Uncle Buddy had seen it jump four rows of corn at a time and later found its tracks in the mud.

Todd floored the four wheeler but the Thang kept up.

Finally, it veered off into a corn field, actually out running the four wheeler. Todd sped home and later drove back with his father to search for tracks but were unable to find any.

He claims that telling the story causes chills to sweep over him, even to this day.

What could this creature be? Some prehistoric man-like animal that escaped evolution in the wilds of Alabama? And how does it sense when someone is about to die?

Its longevity and ability to leap over trailers and rows of corn suggest that it is something supernatural. Perhaps it is a being that has somehow gotten through a puncture in the fabric of time.

Although it has frightened its share of folks, it has never been known to hurt a person or an animal.

Perhaps the civilization of that area of Lawrence County has driven the Hollerin' Thang even further into the woods.

We may never know.

But I would be cautious riding along those dark country roads at night.

RANDOLPH OF THE RITZ

The Ritz Theater, at 103 West Third Street, in downtown Sheffield, opened July 8, 1928, with a bill that included the silent version of *Gentlemen Prefer Blondes*, two serials, and (according to a local newspaper advertisement) "high class music on our Wurlitzer Organ."

The theater was redecorated in the Art Deco style and outfitted for talking pictures in the 1930s.

Until it was closed in the early 1950s, the Ritz showed movies.

On October 27, 1983, the Tennessee Valley Art Association

members hosted a white tie gala, "Evening At The Ritz," amidst the nostalgic ruins of the once grand theater, to kick off the Ritz Restoration Fund Drive. The property had been purchased earlier in the 80s, to be used as the permanent location for Center Stage, the performing arts wing of the Tennessee Valley Art Center.

Soon, the theater had a new heating and air conditioning system, a "loft" proscenium stage, an orchestra pit, dressing rooms, a state of the art lighting system, lobby, modern restroom, and a new ceiling. Comfortable theater seats were refurbished and brought in from the old Tuscumbian Theater. All the renovation was done with the desire to maintain the Art Deco style of the 1920s, while providing a first rate performance center.

The first production, *Anything Goes*, was staged amidst wet paint and piles of sawdust. Still, performers and patrons alike were excited about the work that had gone on in the Ritz. At that time, no one was aware there was a spirit inhabiting the historic theater.

One of the first people to encounter the ghost was Favre Sparks. After one of the rehearsals for *Anything Goes*, Favre was getting ready to lock up for the night. A noise came from the balcony and she looked up to find a man, wearing a dark pinstriped suit, sitting on the second row, second seat of the balcony. Not wanting to lock anyone in, she climbed the stairs to the balcony but no one was there.

Her only explanation was that the theater was haunted, presumably by a man who had worked there in the 20s, or 30s. She did not feel threatened by the spirit and dubbed him Randolph of the Ritz.

Since that time, sightings and encounters with Randolph have been frequent. Nearly everyone who has done a show there has either heard or seen him.

Donna Burns Sparks, who'd performed in and taken part in the production of several plays, had heard tales about Randolph. She'd always considered the Ritz to be her second home and felt comfortable in the old building. When she learned about the resident spirit, it only intrigued her more.

After a rehearsal for *You Can't Take It With You*, Donna and several others were in the dressing room when they heard a crash come from the stage. Upon investigation, they discovered that an empty aquarium had been shattered with a hammer, both of which were being used as props for the play. Donna is not certain whether this was Randolph's handiwork or merely a prank being played by someone who wanted Randolph to take the blame.

The Ritz Theater in Sheffield

He has always been a mischievous entity but also a very protective one. Those who are involved with the Ritz feel his presence is watchful. He seems to stay mostly in the balcony area and in the lighting booth although he has been known to move costumes, much to the annoyance of performers. Costumes are hung from a thirty-foot long rack and sometimes are relocated as much as fifteen feet down the rack. When anyone voices their aggravation at not being able to find their costume, the other performers say, in unison, "Randolph got it."

One night, in February 1991, after a rehearsal for a Gingerbread

Playhouse production, Donna was on the left lip of the stage writing down notes for the following night's rehearsal. Volunteers were busy on the stage, constructing the set. They were using the work lights only to conserve electricity and Donna was having a difficult time seeing her papers. James had been working lights that night from his position in the crow's nest but Donna did not want to bother him to turn on additional lighting.

"I wish I had more light," she mused to herself.

Suddenly, a spot light shone down on her long enough for her to finish what she was writing. She glanced toward the light box and gave James a nod of thanks. The light, then, went out.

After a while, she said something to one of the stage hands about James switching the light on for her. "James?" the surprised stage hand asked. "He couldn't have done it. He left over an hour ago."

Donna laughed out loud. "Well, then," she said, "I feel privileged. I've just had an encounter with Randolph."

Donna isn't the only one who had an experience with Randolph and the lighting. One evening, Terry Pace was locking up for the night. He had turned off all the lights and was just about to close the door when he noticed a faint light coming from the stage. He went back to investigate, squinting and looking up toward the balcony, just catching a glimpse of a man in a pin striped suit, second row, second seat. But before he could get a better look, the light went off, leaving Terry in total darkness.

Donna's husband Jeremy works sound for some of the productions. Often, when wireless microphones are used, the sets worn by the actors mysteriously get dialed in on different frequencies. Perhaps Randolph's energy unintentionally upsets the frequency of the mics.

Everyone who has had encounters with Randolph believe that he is a benign and friendly spirit who looks out for the historic theater.

The Ritz Theater facilities are used by the Tennessee Valley Art Association, but they are also available to other responsible groups, individuals, and organizations.

The Ritz is enjoyed by thousands each year and is a wonderful asset to Shoals heritage and culture. But next time you are enjoying a performance in the building and feel a tingle up your spine when the lights go dark, just remember that Randolph is there, watching the show alongside you.

GEORGE

Norton Auditorium, on the campus of the University of North Alabama, hosts the University's musical and drama productions, as well as lecturers, ceremonies, student events, concerts, and community performances. The building was named for Dr. E. B. Norton, who served as president of the University from 1948, until 1972.

The auditorium was built in the late 1960s, after several Victorian style houses on the site were razed to make room for the expanding university.

Norton Auditorium on the campus of the University of North Alabama

Since Norton was built, students, performers, and professors alike, have had unexplainable experiences in the auditorium. The incidents were attributed to a ghost the drama students dubbed *George*, presumably after a man who died during construction when he tragically fell from scaffolding. No one has actually ever seen the spirit in Norton, so there is no evidence to link the happenings to the *real* George. In fact, the ghost could very well be someone who lived in one of the homes which used to be on the site.

From all accounts, the spirit is a mischievous one.

One night, during a play rehearsal, a sudden, summer storm came up and lighting struck Norton Auditorium. The entire theater filled with smoke. Fire trucks rushed to the scene. After a thorough inspection, it was determined that the air conditioning system had been hit by lightning and that Norton was safe from fire. However, the Fire Marshal asked for two volunteers to spend the night in the building and perform periodic basement to catwalk checks just to scout for any electrical fires that could have been sparked by the lightning.

A young actor, named David, and one of his friends quickly raised their hands for the assignment, all but forgetting about the building's reputation for being haunted.

"Here are a couple of flashlights," the fireman said as he thrust them into David's hands. "We're just gonna cut the breakers off to be on the safe side."

David and his friend exchanged worried glances. Perhaps they'd bitten off more than they could chew. Still, they bravely settled in on the stage, armed with only their flashlights and the emergency house lights.

An eerie haze of smoke still floated, ghostlike, over the entire darkened theater. And although they were spooked by the quiet solitude and the acrid smelling mist, David and his friend made their rounds, up into the balcony area, down into the basement, up high above the stage onto the catwalk, with only the feeble light of a flashlight to guide them. No mention of George was made, but his presence weighed heavily on their minds. Especially as the emergency house lights began to grow dimmer and dimmer.

Around 3 a.m., both boys decided to get some sleep. David's friend stretched out on the stage and fell asleep almost immediately. David, however, lay awake in the looming darkness, his ears trained on the pops and groans of the big, empty, auditorium, his gaze fixed on the shadows overhead.

Suddenly, a noise came from the catwalk and David sat bolt upright, shining the weak beam of his flashlight upward. The catwalk shook, the metallic sound echoing throughout the empty auditorium, and then a commotion David described as sounding like a covey of birds taking flight all at once reverberated off the walls. David elbowed his friend just as Norton Auditorium blazed to life, the entire building illuminated as every light in the house came on at once.

Both boys raced to the breaker box, thinking someone had come in and switched them on. But the main switch was still OFF.

David and his friend spent the rest of the night on the steps outside the stage door.

During a rehearsal for *Six Characters In Search of an Author*, drama student, Laura Connolly, was taking notes for director, Robert Allen Holder. No one was in the light booth but, strangely, the lights kept coming on and going off, seemingly of their own accord. Suddenly, one burst, raining fragments down on the stage. According to Laura, Robert Allen Holder said, "I told you there's something in here."

Veteran stage actor, Kyle Weir, has also had encounters with George. During a production of Christopher Marlowe's *Dr. Faustus*, there seemed to be a pall over the entire production. According to legend the play itself, is actually cursed. Add that to an already mischievous spirit, and the end result is disaster. Everything that could have possibly gone wrong on opening night, did go wrong.

Kyle played several characters in the play, one of which was a servant. As he was standing backstage, awaiting his cue to carry out a tray of chalices, another actor brushed past him. Suddenly, all the glasses began to sway and all but one fell to the stage and broke.

An unexplainable extra character dressed in monk's robes was witnessed on the stage.

And during rehearsals, several of the actors stopped to gaze up into the catwalk, from which strange noises emanated.

The catwalk has been the scene of many of George's pranks. Terry Pace was performing in a play directed by Jim Davis when the distinct sound of footsteps was heard overhead on the catwalk. All the actors were accounted for on the stage. Still, Jim Davis peered up into the darkness and ordered the culprit to come down. No sound was heard for a moment and then the footsteps began again.

"It's dangerous up there!" Jim called into the shadows. "Whoever you are, just come down."

The footsteps sounded again and this time, Jim sent Terry and one other actor up each side of the stairs leading to the catwalk. These stairs are the only way up or down from the catwalk and no one had come down them. When Terry and the other actor reached the top, the catwalk was empty. It was then, that someone noticed a shadowy, human-sized figure in the alcove overlooking the stage. Jim Davis yelled at it and instantly, it shot across the theater in mid-air and disappeared behind the organ pipes.

George, it seems, performs most of his antics during plays. Although he has frightened his share of drama students, he has never done anything to actually hurt anyone. Perhaps he merely wishes to audition for a part.

If you perchance see a show in Norton, glance up at the alcove when the houselights go down. You just might catch a glimpse of George.

HAUNTED FLORENCE CEMETERY

A stroll through the Florence Cemetery is like taking a walk through history. In fact, through the efforts of Bob Torbert and Lee Freeman, the cemetery was added to the Alabama State Register of Historic Places.

Located at the corner of Dr. Hicks Boulevard and Tennessee Street, the cemetery was laid out by Italian surveyor, Ferdinand Sannoner, in his plans for the city.

Historic Florence Cemetery

Over nine thousand graves, dating from approximately 1818, dot the gently undulating hills. Among them, two of the five Alabama governors from Lauderdale County, some of Florence's earliest settlers, soldiers who died during the Civil War, several prominent community leaders, and some say the most infamous criminal to have ever lived in Northwest Alabama.

Graves of two former Alabama Governors, Edward Asbury O'Neal and Emmet O'Neal

Tombstones and monuments often tell the story of the person buried beneath them. For instance, an anchor on the stone signifies the person is at rest. A book with a cross shows they possessed faith. Ivy indicates immortality. Oak leaves are sign of victory. A lily means the person was pure. A torch suggests immortality if turned up, and if turned down, a life cut short. A stone carved to look like a tree, utilized by the Woodmen of the World symbolizes a life cut short. A lamb signifies innocence and usually marks the graves of children.

The oldest known grave in the cemetery belongs to Mary Nichols Evans (1763-1825). She was the mother of Florence's first mayor, Alexander H. Wood, who also rests in the cemetery.

Songwriter, Arthur Alexander (1940-1993), who penned *You Better Move On*, and who was covered by The Rolling Stones, George Jones, and The Beatles is interred there.

Reverend Hiram Kennedy-Douglass (1893-1975), who donated the fountain in Wilson Park, hosted a classical music hour on WLAY, and was a leading patron in the arts, lies in the Florence Cemetery.

The first father/son governors in the State of Alabama, Edward Asbury O'Neal (1819-1890), and his son Emmet O'Neal (1854-1922), are among the prominent Florence citizens who rest on the site.

The only stone set at an unusual angle (not directly East to West) belongs to Susan Rapier (1811-1841). She was a *free woman of color* who married a former slave, John H. Rapier, Sr. (1808-1869). After the death of river merchant, Richard Rapier, John was awarded his freedom, and he became the city's first African American barber. He amassed such wealth that he was able to send his sons James Thomas and John Jr. to the Buxton Academy in Canada.

When Susan died in 1841, because of John's wealth and connections, she was buried in the "white" section of the cemetery. However, her stone placed at an angle, presumably to differentiate her graves from the others.

Her sons went on to achieve prominence. John Rapier Jr. became a surgeon for the Federal Army during the Civil War, and, in 1873, James Thomas Rapier became the second African American from Alabama to be elected to Congress.

In Section S-1, Row 7, lie two (possibly four) of the six Lauderdale

County, African American men who served in the Confederate Army. Reuben Patterson (1836-1928), who served as body servant to Col. Josiah Patterson of the 5th Alabama Cavalry, CSA, in addition to his duty as bugler, and unofficial "horse swapper." The other known soldier is George Washington "Wash" Seawright (1848-1931), who served as body servant for Mitchell "Mike" Malone of the 4th Alabama Cavalry, CSA.

The grave of Susan Rapier is the only one in the Florence Cemetery set at an angle

Contractor, Zebulon Pike Morrison (1818-1895), rests in the Florence Cemetery. A former Florence mayor, he built the Florence Female Academy (Florence Synodical College), Wesleyan Hall on the University of North Alabama campus, and several others in Florence.

One of the most interesting monuments in the cemetery is the Sallie Garibaldi Memorial Mausoleum. An Italian immigrant, John Garibaldi (1855-1939) came to Florence in 1888, where he opened a harness and shoemaking shop of the corner of East Tennessee Street and Seminary Street. In 1914, he opened a lunch café at Court and Mobile Streets. He married Sallie Bernard (1865-1934), and the couple had two children who passed away between 1900 and 1910. Each year, children's toys were placed in the top of the Garibaldi mausoleum in memory of the children.

Garibaldi Mausoleum where toys were placed in memory of the Garibaldis' children

One of the area's wealthiest businessmen, Frances Marion "Frank" Perry, Sr. (1845-1929) lies in Section K-2, Row 1. After relocating to Lauderdale County in 1866, he settled in Oakland and quickly accrued such a large fortune that rumors spread that he was actually the outlaw, Frank James.

Graves in Soldiers' Rest

Local lore suggests that one heinous criminal was so despised that he was not permitted to be buried within the walls of the cemetery. His name was Thomas Marion Clark (1828-1872), and he first settled in the Jacksonburg community about six miles north of Florence. After allegedly joining both the Confederate and Federal Armies during the Civil War, he deserted, made his way back to the Shoals Area, and formed a gang of bushwhackers that tortured, killed, and robbed the citizens of North Alabama and Middle Tennessee during and after the Civil War.

On September 3, 1872, Clark was apprehended by City Marshal William Edward Blair (1847-1894), along with two other Bugger Gang members, Gibson and Davenport.

The three were removed from the jail by a lynch mob and hanged in a vacant lot on Pine Street behind the Masonic Lodge Hall. Clark had bragged that he killed eighteen men in his lifetime, and one child. He boasted "no one will ever run over me!" So legend has it that Clark was buried beneath Tennessee Street, just outside the cemetery gates.

Clark's exploits are detailed in *Bugger Saga: The Civil War Story of Guerilla and Bushwhacker Warfare in Lauderdale County, Alabama and Southern Middle Tennessee,* by Wade Pruitt. The book is based on folklore and stories told to Pruitt by his ancestors.

On the Southern end of the cemetery, beneath the shade of ancient cedars, is an area known as Soldiers' Rest. This area was used to bury war casualties after a skirmish on the streets of Florence in 1862. Many known—and unknown—soldiers are buried here.

Among them lies Colonel Samuel Spenser Ives (1836-1917), who served in Company I, 9th Alabama Infantry, CSA, prior to joining

Company A, 35th Alabama Infantry, CSA. Wounded five times at the 1864 Battle of Franklin, he carried nine bullets to his grave at the time of his death in 1917.

It seems not all those buried in Soldiers' Rest are at peace.

Visitors to the historic cemetery have witnessed a misty apparition floating amidst the soldiers' graves.

Two women, paying their respects to a deceased ancestor near Soldiers' Rest, saw what appeared to be fog drifting between the graves. At first, they thought it odd, but then found it alarming when they realized the day was too hot, and the hour too late for fog.

When the mist did not dissipate, they got in their car and promptly left!

One woman claims to have seen the ghost of a forlorn man in Civil War uniform standing amongst the soldiers' graves.

Still others have felt inexplicable chills in the vicinity, even on hot, humid days.

Perhaps the spirit is that of one of the unknown soldiers, far from home, still worried that his family may not know what awful fate befell him.

An Unknown Confederate Soldier's Grave in the Florence Cemetery

POPE'S TAVERN

Pope's Tavern Museum is arguably the oldest structure in the city of Florence, Alabama. Some believe it was built as a stagecoach stop around 1811, by a Scot named Christopher Cheatham, who ran it for Leroy Pope. General Andrew Jackson stopped at the tavern in 1814, *en route* to battle the British in New Orleans. His army camped on the surrounding grounds in the vicinity of the tavern.

Pope's Tavern in the 1930s

The house was first used as a hospital during the Civil War following a skirmish on the corner of Court and Tuscaloosa streets in Florence, Alabama. During the war, there was a livery stable on the site. Several Yankees took refuge in it. To smoke them out, the Confederates threw lighted pine knot torches onto the shingle roof of the building and set the stable on fire. The Yankees fled brandishing a white flag and bringing their wounded with them.

The wounded from both sides were brought to Pope's Tavern and placed side by side on improvised cots and pallets. At that time, there were few available doctors and most of the nursing was done by the women of Florence. Among the nurses was Pauline Stewart, her daughter, Mrs. Cutler Smith, and Olivia O'Neal, the wife of General Edward O'Neal of the 26th Alabama Infantry.

After a bloody cavalry skirmish at Elk River, east of Florence, the wounded from both sides were, again, brought to Pope's Tavern.

One Union soldier, Ogilvie E. Hamblin, a private in Company E of the 2nd Michigan Cavalry, was guarding Florence under the command of Brigadier General John Thomas Croxton, when Confederate General John Bell Hood brought his beleaguered Army of Tennessee across the Tennessee River on the way to the Battle of Franklin.

On October 30th, 1864, Hamblin's company encountered Confederate Brigadier General Jacob Hunter Sharps' Mississippians on the north bank of the Tennessee River. Hamblin's men were routed and retreated. Hamblin, himself, was shot in the left arm and captured. The Confederates marched him to Pope's Tavern where his arm was amputated the following day.

After Hamblin recovered sufficiently, he was sent to the General Hospital in Columbus, Mississippi, where he convalesced for six weeks. Later, he was transferred to Cahaba Prison Camp, near Selma, Alabama.

On March 15, 1865, Hamblin was exchanged, and along with 1,866 other ex-prisoners of war, he was sent to Vicksburg, Mississippi, to await transportation to his northern home.

A large portion of these ex-prisoners were slated to travel on the Sultana, a typical side-wheel steamer built in Cincinnati, in 1863, to haul cotton on the lower Mississippi. The Sultana was registered at 1719 tons and had a crew of 85. Her captain was the competent and experienced, J. C. Mason of St. Louis. For two years, the Sultana had carried cotton between New Orleans and St. Louis. She also frequently transported Union army personnel.

On April 21, 1865, the Sultana left New Orleans, with about 100 cabin passengers, and a cargo which included sugar and assorted livestock. By law, she could carry 376 passengers, including her crew.

A few hours before reaching Vicksburg, a leak developed along a joint of one of the Sultana's boilers. A quick repair job was made by putting on a "soft-patch," of quarter inch iron plate.

After arriving in Vicksburg, soldiers eager to return home began boarding the Sultana in droves, quickly exceeding her capacity. In all, some 1800 – 2000 ex-prisoners boarded her, and, in addition, two companies of soldiers were brought aboard. Altogether, there were about 2300 passengers on the steamer when she cast off—six times as many as the steamer was designed to carry.

The Sultana pulled away and headed upstream against a current made stronger than usual by the river's flood state.

She docked in Memphis and some of the passengers went ashore. Some of her cargo was also unloaded. The boiler was repaired again and the Sultana's big paddlewheels began propelling the dreadfully overloaded steamer upriver toward Cairo.

Around 2:00 a.m., the leaky boilers exploded. The blast was heard as far away as Memphis. Steamers quickly headed upriver to offer assistance.

Half the vessel disintegrated. Hundreds of sleeping soldiers were hurtled into the water along with twisted remnants of machinery, fragments of wood, furniture, and deck beams.

Private Hamblin helped to open a hatch that saved the lives of soldiers trapped there. He was rescued several miles from the site of the explosion, found clinging to a tree branch he had managed to grab with his one arm.

Many of those on board the Sultana could not swim and remained on the burning hulk. Others leaped into the water. One survivor recalled: "The men who were afraid to take to the water could be seen clinging to the sides of the bow of the boat until they were singed off like flies."

This photo was taken April 26, 1865, one day before the Sultana sank into the Mississippi River

After the remains of the boat washed ashore on a small island, the Sultana sank, hissing and steaming as the hulk descended into the dark waters of the Mississippi.

When dawn came, survivors were scattered down the river all the way to Memphis, clinging to logs, barrels, sections of railing, anything that would keep them afloat. One Confederate soldier is said to have rescued fifteen Union soldiers single-handedly.

For many days after the accident, a barge was sent out to pick up dead bodies in the Mississippi. It is estimated that between 1500 – 1900 men were killed on the most terrible steamship disaster in history.

Private Ogilvie Hamblin was discharged in July and returned to his home in Pulaski, Michigan.

One Florence doctor who treated soldiers at Pope's Tavern, and who came from a prominent Florence family, worked as a spy for the Yankees.

His name was Dr. Hugh McVay and he was related to the former Alabama governor, who bore the same name, Hugh McVay, and who served a very brief term as governor of the state from July 17, 1837, until November 22, 1837.

Dr. McVay certainly held sympathy for the Union cause. In his Official Records report, of January 23, 1864, Union Brigadier General Grenville M. Dodge writes to Lieutenant Colonel Phillips in Athens: *"Dr. McVay says a force from Bainbridge passed up the Waterville road on Wednesday night. They went 15 miles and were still going on. How many men do you want to go down and clean out this band of rebels, and how many can you take from your command?"*

Dr. McVay was a frequent visitor of the Union Captain A. P. Hall, who convalesced under the care of Pauline Stewart and her daughter, Ophelia Smith, at their home on Court Street.

In 1863, Hall, who was a member of the 7th Illinois Regiment commanded by Colonel Rowett, heard that several horses had been hidden about 14 miles out of Florence on Butler Creek. He took his men to confiscate the horses and encountered a group of Southern bushwhackers. A skirmish ensued and Hall was wounded. He was brought back to Florence and taken to the Stewart home where he was attended by General Sherman's medics. Upon examination, it was determined he would not survive.

The Stewart women nursed Hall until his death, about month later, and then had him buried in the Florence cemetery, where his body remained until it was disinterred, by order of the War Department, and removed to the National Cemetery at Corinth, Mississippi.

Before Hall's death, he was visited several times by Dr. Hugh McVay. Hall gave McVay his boots who sold them to Mrs. Sample for $10.00. She gave them to her brother who was a Confederate soldier.

Civil War medical care was primitive by modern standards.

Sanitation was rare and cleanliness was often an afterthought. Instruments were never sterilized and were often used over and over again as doctors moved from patient to patient. Gangrene, tetanus and blood poisoning were common, as were many contagious diseases such as typhoid and dysentery.

Treatment was equally primitive. Wounds were bathed in unsterilized cold water to relieve the sensation of burning, and amputation was the typical way of dealing with wounds in the arms and legs. As for drugs, that which was available — chloroform for operations; morphine and laudanum for pain relief — was highly addictive and often poorly administered. Demand for these drugs and treatment often quickly exceeded supply, especially after major battles.

Although treatment improved as the war progressed, the quality of care remained low, and many patients died as much from the treatment they received as from the wounds they sustained or the diseases they contracted.

Pope's Tavern remained a hospital until after the surrender of Lee at Appomattox. Thirty-three soldiers were known to have died there and countless others underwent surgery there.

Ophelia Smith, in her memoir of the Civil War, wrote: *"In our hospital here, in 1862, the sick soldiers were brought from Forts Henry and Donelson after their fall, and as well as I can remember, there were 700 of them and out of this number 32 died and were buried in the Florence Cemetery along with two others that were killed in a skirmish about 4 miles from the city by General Rowett's command in 1865."*

Pope's Tavern is still standing and now serves Florence as a museum. Many Civil War artifacts are on display there, including: the flag carried by Charles Daniel Stewart with the 4th Alabama Infantry Regiment at the Battle of Bull Run, the coat worn by General Edward Asbury O'Neal during the Civil War, and the saw used by wartime surgeons to amputate wounded limbs.

Pope's Tavern is also home to more than one ghost. One tour guide who worked in the house, often experienced cold drafts in the house and heard the door opening as if visitors had arrived, however, when she went to look, no one was there.

Ophelia and Cutler Smith

Visitors from all over the United States come to Pope's Tavern Museum, and often, some of these sightseers, who have thoroughly been enjoying a tour of the house, arrive in, what is now, the bedroom, only to experience feelings of apprehension, nausea, and terror. Usually, they will have to leave the room—but they always describe their experiences the same way. They report hearing the sounds of men screaming in agony and of smelling the stench of rot and metallic tang of blood.

Curiously, the bedroom was the room used for the surgeries during the Civil War.

One man, who worked on Civil War uniforms was asked to restore the coat of General O'Neal. He arrived at the tavern late one evening and went to work repairing O'Neal's jacket. And then, he heard the sound of footsteps coming slowly up the stairs and then down the hallway toward the room where he was. Getting the feeling someone did not want him in the house, he collected his things and left.

The next night, he returned with a friend. And then, both heard the heavy footsteps ascending the stairs—and both rushed to get out of the house.

One evening during the *Haunted History of the Shoals Ghost Walk Tours*, while the tour guide was telling the history of the tavern, a loud knock came from inside the building—long after the alarm had been set. One unlucky fellow on the tour, Brad Osborne, actually passed out during the tour in 2010, upon hearing the stories of the wounded in Pope's Tavern. He described having feelings of overwhelming sadness when the guide told of the surgeries Civil War soldiers suffered in the tavern.

Pope's Tavern Museum today

During a garden club meeting, all the ladies were seated around an antique tavern table when a loud, cracking, an unexplainable pop came from the room which had been used for the surgeries.

David Hope was in the museum, during the hours of operation, working on an informational DVD on the historic markers of Florence. As he was telling the history of Pope's Tavern, the hotel bell set out by the museum director at the time, Jo Parkhurst, to alert her to visitors to the museum, rang.

David looked at the bell. He knew no one had rung it. The camera man asked, "Did you hear that?" And then Jo, who was giving a tour in the parlor called, "I'll be with you in a moment."

David merely stared at the bell. For all in the tavern had heard it—however, no one had rung it.

No doubt, the spirits at Pope's Tavern are associated with the turbulent years of the Civil War and approve of its status as a museum. But the ancient walls hold miseries only few can imagine. Those who have avoid the Civil War hospital turned museum at all costs.

PLACES OF INTEREST

Florence / Lauderdale Tourism
200 Jim Spain Drive
Florence, AL 35630
(256) 740-4141

Pope's Tavern Museum
203 Hermitage Drive
Florence, AL 35630
(256) 760-6439

Florence Cemetery
705 East College Street
Florence, AL 35630

Pickett Place Event Venue
438 North Seminary
Florence, AL 35630
(256) 366-2925

Ritz Theater
111 West Third Street
Sheffield, AL
(256) 381-8370

HAUNTED HISTORY OF THE SHOALS GHOST WALK TOUR

A spine chilling night awaits you in the company of a masterful storyteller who will entertain you with tales steeped in legend, folklore, and truth.

As twilight creeps over the homes and hidden courtyards of historic downtown Florence, prepare yourself to witness the mysterious and inexplicable.

Each year, during the week of Halloween, Debra conducts the Haunted History of the Shoals Ghost Walk Tour.

Souls depart at 7:30 pm, from Wilson Park in Historic Downtown Florence.

Tours last 90 minutes and cover approximately 1 mile.

Reservations are not required.

Visit www.FlorenceGhostWalk for more information, or to contact Debra.

Other Northwest Alabama Haunted Attractions:

Arx Mortis Haunted House
4051 Hwy. 72
Killen, AL 35645

WHERE DEBRA'S OTHER BOOKS CAN BE FOUND

Florence / Lauderdale Tourism
200 Jim Spain Drive
Florence, Alabama 35630
(256) 740-4141

Cold Water Bookstore
101 W. Sixth St
Tuscumbia, Alabama
(256) 381-2525

Ye Ole General Store
219 N Seminary St
Florence, Alabama 35630
(256) 764-0601

Lawrence County Archives
2588 Hwy 43 S
Leoma, TN 38468
(931) 852-4091

www.Amazon.com

ABOUT THE AUTHOR

DEBRA GLASS is the author of more than thirty five books. Since childhood she has been fascinated by things that go bump in the night. While writing True Shoals Ghost Stories Vol. 1, she realized many of the hauntings occurred in her hometown of Florence, Alabama, and decided to start a ghost walk tour. Since its beginnings in 2002, the Haunted History of the Shoals Ghost Walk Tour has become a perennial favorite during the Halloween season.

Debra lives in Alabama with her family, two smart-alec ghosts, and a glaring of diabolical black cats.

Other folklore collections by Debra Glass include:

True Shoals Ghost Stories Vol. 1

True Shoals Ghost Stories Vol. 3

Skeletons on Campus – True Ghost Stories of Alabama Colleges and Universities

Skeletons of the Civil War – True Ghost Stories of the Army of Tennessee

Haunted Mansions in the Heart of Dixie

Young Adult Paranormal Romance

Eternal

Debra conducts the Haunted History of the Shoals Ghost Walk Tour annually during the week of Halloween. For more information about Debra, her books, and her tour, check out her website: www.FlorenceGhostWalk.com